Biblical Wisdom to Transform Your Marriage

Dr. Marcus Peter

En Route Books and Media, LLC
Saint Louis, MO

En Route Books and Media, LLC
5705 Rhodes Avenue
St. Louis, MO 63109

Contact us at
contactus@enroutebooksandmedia.com

Cover Credit: Marcus Peter

ISBN-13: 979-8-88870-538-4
Library of Congress Control Number:
Available online at https://catalog.loc.gov

Table of Contents

Chapter 1: Satan's 12 Attacks on Marriage 1

Spiritual Warfare, the Fall, and the Defence of the Covenant 1
Creation, Human Dignity, and Why Satan Hates Marriage 2
The Primordial Structure of Society 5
The Subtlety of the Serpent 7
"Where Are You?" 9
The Blame Game and the Mercy of God 10
Twelve Common Attacks on Marriage 12
The Book of Tobit and the Defence of Marriage 18
The Weapons of Warfare 19
Claim the Grace and Fight Together 20
Meditation Questions 22
Call to Action 23

Chapter 2: Biblical Wisdom for Husbands 25

Dying to Self, Living for Christ, and Bringing Heaven into the Home 25
The Premise: Heaven Through Suffering 26
The Lie of the Culture About Marriage 29
Baptism, Spiritual Marriage, and the Wedding Feast of the Lamb 30

Small Acts, Hidden Holiness, and the Sanctification of the Household 32
Men, Lead the Charge 33
A Happy Marriage in a Broken World 35
The Groom in Black 37
Generativity, Receptivity, and the Life of Heaven in the Home 39
Heaven Can Be Born in the Family 41
Be Romantic, Become Holy 42
Meditation Questions 43
Call to Action 44

Chapter 3: Biblical Wisdom for Wives 45

Woman as Helpmate, Remedy, and Strength in the Covenant 45
The Woman as God's Help in the Household 46
Marriage as a Participation in Trinitarian Life 49
The Long History of Failure in Salvation History 51
Eve and the Silent Husband 53
Noah, Abraham, Moses, and David 54
The Call to Mutual Sanctification 57
The Wife's Vow and the Gift of the Person ... 59
Twelve Ways Satan Attacks Wives 60
Presence, Tenderness, and the Domestic Covenant 65
A Wife's First Priorities 66

Final Exhortation to Wives 67
Meditation Questions 69
Call to Action 70

Chapter 4: Satan's Attack on Marital Intimacy 71

Satan's Attack on Marital Intimacy 71
The Curse After the Fall and What It Actually Means 72
The Sorrow of Childbearing and the Wounding of a Good Gift 75
Adam's Failure and the Curse on the Ground 76
What Satan Could Not Curse 78
Marital Intimacy as Sign, Pledge, and Sanctifying Grace 80
God in the Room 82
The Song of Songs and the Language of Holy Desire 84
Why the Devil Targets the Bed 85
Ten Ways Satan Attacks Marital Intimacy 86
Purifying the Imagination 91
Marital Intimacy and the Renewal of Vows ... 92
Go Be Saints 93
Meditation Questions 94
Call to Action 96

Marriage Checkpoint Questionnaire 97
Instructions 97

Marriage Checkpoint 99
A Couple's Shared Examination of Covenant Life 99
Christ at the Center 99
Communication and Emotional Unity 99
Love, Tenderness, and Affection 100
Conflict and Reconciliation 100
Intimacy and Purity 101
Shared Life and Mission 101
Notes on How to Use It Together 102

Reflection Prompts After the Questionnaire 104
Simple Scoring Guide 104
Final Question 105

Chapter 1

Satan's 12 Attacks on Marriage

Spiritual Warfare, the Fall, and the Defence of the Covenant

I suspect that many of you are reading this book because the topic struck something in you. You saw the words Satan's attack on marriage and you realised that even if you have never explicitly named it in those terms, there is something deeply true about it. There is an elephant in the room, and it ought to be spoken aloud plainly.

Here it is.

Whether you like it or not, two things are true. Your marriage is spiritual warfare. Satan is coming after your marriage. And men, ordinarily he will go through our brides to get to us, because that is one of the first patterns established in Scripture.

That is where we must begin, because unless we understand the battle, we will keep misreading the symptoms. There are patterns of affliction, confusion, fracture, and spiritual erosion that keep showing up in modern marriages, and they are far too consistent to dismiss as mere coincidence. I have seen these patterns in hosting my programme, in travelling, in preaching, and in listening to countless stories from couples and families. I have also been helped by the wisdom of Greg and Lisa Popcak, whose practical pastoral insights have served many families well. My purpose here is not to pretend to be a psychologist. I am not going to do that. I want instead to speak from a biblical and theological perspective, and to show how Satan attacks marriage and what Christians can do spiritually to fight back.

Knowing the battle is half the battle. Strategising and engaging the battle is the other half.

Creation, Human Dignity, and Why Satan Hates Marriage

To understand why marriage is such a prime target, we must go back to Genesis. In the first creation account, the human person appears at the climax of creation. "So God created man in his own image, in the image of God he created him; male and female he created them" (Gen 1:27). In the second creation account, man is formed first, then the garden is prepared, then the animals are brought forth, and finally woman is created from man's side (Gen 2:7, 18–23). These accounts do not contradict each other. They illuminate different facets of the same truth.

In the first account, the inspired author shows us that God saved the best for last. In the second, he shows us that the best was present at the beginning and crowned again at the end. Saint John Paul II, in his catecheses later collected as the Theology of the Body, drew significant attention to the second account precisely because it reveals the distinct personal meaning of man and woman.

So I often put it like this. Man is the crowning authority of visible creation, and woman is the crown jewel. In man there is a certain dominion within creation, and in woman the dignity of that dominion shines forth in a unique and personal way. Both are made in the image of God. Both possess equal dignity. Yet they are not interchangeable.

The Catechism teaches, "Of all visible creatures only man is 'able to know and love his creator'" (CCC

356). It goes on to affirm that man and woman together are willed by God in equality and complementarity (CCC 369–373). The human being therefore occupies a strange and glorious place in creation. We are bodily creatures, and therefore share something with animals. Yet we also possess rational souls, intellect, and will, and therefore stand in a unique relation to the spiritual order. Saint Thomas Aquinas explains that the human soul is spiritual and immortal, capable of knowing truth and loving the good in a way no merely material creature can do (Summa Theologiae I, q. 75, aa. 2–6).

Humanity therefore stands at the meeting point of matter and spirit. We are, in that sense, a bridge between the material and the immaterial, the earthly and the heavenly. That is part of what makes our dignity so singular. It is also part of what makes us hated by Satan.

If Scripture is taken seriously, then the devil's rebellion is bound up with pride, refusal, and hatred of the order God established. The Epistle to the Hebrews says that angels are "ministering spirits sent forth to serve, for the sake of those who are to obtain salvation" (Heb 1:14). In Catholic theology, guardian angels are truly given to serve and guard us. The idea that exalted spiritual beings attend lowly embodied creatures is itself humiliating to demonic pride. Add to this the astonishing claim of Saint Paul that "we are to judge angels" (1 Cor 6:3), and one begins to grasp why the demonic hatred of the human person is so intense.

Satan hates man because man bears the divine image. Satan hates marriage because marriage is the primordial form of human communion. Satan hates male and female because their complementarity reflects the wisdom of God and opens into fruitfulness, family, and covenant.

The Primordial Structure of Society

Genesis 2 culminates in language that the Hebrew people understood as covenantal and nuptial. Adam receives the woman and says, "This at last is bone of my bones and flesh of my flesh" (Gen 2:23). The text then declares, "Therefore a man leaves his father and his mother and cleaves to his wife, and they become one flesh" (Gen 2:24). Christ himself later cites this text and confirms its permanent authority: "What therefore God has joined together, let no man put asunder" (Matt 19:6).

The Hebrew imagination would not have read Genesis 2 as a vague romantic scene. It is the establishment of marriage at the beginning of human history. In that sense marriage is primordial. It is the foundational structure of human society, preceding state, economy, institution, and civil law. The family is not an invention of culture. It is built into creation.

The Second Vatican Council calls the family "the first and vital cell of society" (Apostolicam Actuositatem, 11). The Catechism teaches that the family is the original cell of social life and the domestic church (CCC 2207; 1655–1658). So if Satan wants to destroy society, he will come after the first cell. If he wants to deform humanity, he will attack manhood, womanhood, marriage, and the family. That is not speculative. It is logical.

This is why attacks on male and female, on marriage, and on the integrity of the body are never merely sociological. They are spiritual. I would say plainly that the transgender ideology, in its attempt to dissolve the givenness of male and female, is a profoundly disordered rebellion against created reality. It seeks to erase the stable grammar of the human person. John Paul II spoke of the "masculine" and "feminine genius," meaning that masculinity and femininity are not merely external or accidental, though they reach into the personal being of man and woman (Mulieris Dignitatem, 29–31). The body matters. Biology matters. Yet personhood is more than a mechanism. There is something in the soul itself that corresponds to the truth of being male or female.

To attack that difference is to attack the foundation of marriage itself. Dissolve the meaning of male and female, and the institution of marriage soon follows. Dissolve marriage, and the family becomes unstable. Dissolve the family, and society loses the very structure by which love, authority, sacrifice, and belonging are ordinarily learned.

The Subtlety of the Serpent

Now we turn to Genesis 3. "Now the serpent was more subtle than any other wild creature that the

Lord God had made" (Gen 3:1). The subtlety here matters. Evil does not usually present itself in recognisably monstrous form. If it did, most people would recoil. Mother Teresa once made observations to this effect, namely that if we saw evil in its full ugliness, we would run from it. Satan works through insinuation, repackaging, euphemism, and seduction.

C. S. Lewis made a similar point in Mere Christianity, that one of the devil's great successes is persuading people that he is not real. If he can hide himself behind systems, desires, trends, or feelings, then his work proceeds all the more easily.

Genesis 3 is especially revealing because Satan's first move is theological before it becomes moral. He comes against the intimacy of man and woman with God. In the Hebrew text, the distinction between divine names helps illuminate this. The covenant name, often represented in English as LORD in capital letters, corresponds to *Yahweh*, the God who has entered intimate relationship with us. Other names such as *Elohim* emphasise transcendence and majesty. The serpent subtly shifts the horizon. He draws Eve away from God as an intimate covenant Lord and toward God conceived as distant authority. The temptation is therefore not only "Take the fruit." It is also "Lose the relationship. Reinterpret God. Distrust the Father."

That remains one of Satan's first moves in any marriage. He comes first against intimacy with God. Once that is weakened, the rest becomes easier.

"Where Are You?"

After the fall, the Lord God walks in the garden and calls to the man, "Where are you?" (Gen 3:9). That question is not geographical. God is not playing hide-and-seek. He is asking about Adam's interior state. Where are you spiritually? Where are you morally? Where are you in relation to me, to your bride, to your vocation?

That same question is posed to every husband and every marriage. God walks through the cool of the garden of our homes and asks, especially of the husband, "Where are you?" The state of that answer will often determine the state of the marriage.

Men must hear this clearly. Satan commonly gets to the husband by first destabilising the bride and the home around him. That is already visible in Genesis.

Eve is approached first. Yet Adam is "with her" (Gen 3:6). He is present. He is silent. He fails to protect. He fails to intervene. He fails in covenantal headship. He receives from Eve what he was meant to guard her against.

This is why I am often hard on men. It is not because I think men have it easy. I do not. It is because the urgency of male vocation is so intense in a culture that despises and misunderstands it. If men do not rise into their God-given role as protector, provider, priestly presence, and servant leader, then the marriage will suffer badly. Ephesians 5 remains decisive here: "Husbands, love your wives, as Christ loved the church and gave himself up for her" (Eph 5:25). This is sacrificial headship, not domination. It is cruciform authority.

The Blame Game and the Mercy of God

When God confronts Adam, Adam does not confess simply. Instead he says, "The woman whom thou gavest to be with me, she gave me fruit of the tree, and I ate" (Gen 3:12). There is almost a bitter sarcasm in it. Adam blames Eve, and beneath that, he blames God. Eve then blames the serpent: "The serpent beguiled me, and I ate" (Gen 3:13). Neither fully owns the sin.

This is an ancient human instinct. We pass the moral buck. We explain, justify, and redirect. Yet God, in one of the most astonishing turns in all of Scripture, takes the burden of redemption onto himself. He addresses the serpent and declares, "I will put enmity between you and the woman, and between your seed and her seed; he shall crush your head, and you shall bruise his heel" (Gen 3:15).

This is the Protoevangelium, the first Gospel. The woman will become part of the devil's defeat. The seed will come through her. The serpent will wound, though he will be destroyed in the process. The Fathers saw here the first promise of Christ and Mary, the New Adam and the New Eve. The Catechism explicitly teaches that this passage announces the Messiah and his Mother, and that Mary is the "New Eve" whose obedience unties the knot of Eve's disobedience (CCC 410–411).

This matters for marriage because it shows us the pattern of redemption. Christ overcomes evil not by evasion, though by sacrificial love. He takes the blow in order to crush the head of the serpent. That becomes the model for spouses as well. Marriage is saved through self-giving, repentance, forgiveness, sacramental grace, and the courage to die to self.

Twelve Common Attacks on Marriage

What follows is not exhaustive, though it does reflect some of the most recurring patterns visible in modern life.

1. Divorce normalised as an escape hatch

> Modern culture has psychologically built divorce into the structure of expectation. Covenant has been replaced by contingency. Yet marriage is not an exchange of goods and services. It is a total gift of self. The Catechism teaches that the marriage bond is established by God himself and that a valid sacramental marriage is indissoluble (CCC 1640; 2382–2386).

2. Pornography

Pornography has no place in marriage. It damages the imagination, distorts perception, trains the eye to consume rather than reverence, and invites grave spiritual darkness. Christ says, "Every one who looks at a woman lustfully has already committed adultery with her in his heart" (Matt 5:28). The Catechism calls pornography a grave offense because it perverts the conjugal act and harms all involved (CCC 2354).

3. Radical self-focus

Modern expressive individualism teaches that marriage exists to fulfil the self. Yet the Christian vision is the opposite. Marriage is ordered to self-gift. Fulton Sheen put it well: if one expects from the spouse what only God can give, disappointment becomes inevitable. The spouse is not God. The spouse is a gift and companion on the way to God.

4. Sexual confusion

The attempted redefinition of marriage, the loss of complementarity, homosexual ideology, and transgender ideology all converge in an assault on male and female. They seek to erase the givenness of the body and the covenantal meaning of sexual difference.

5. The contraceptive mentality

This is deeper than the use of contraception itself. It is a way of thinking that sees children as threats, burdens, or obstacles. Humanae Vitae insists that the unitive and procreative meanings of the marital act must not be severed (HV 12). Every child is to be received as a gift, not as intrusion.

6. Busyness, exhaustion, and distraction

Social media, endless entertainment, doomscrolling, fatigue, overwork, and constant stimulation destroy attentiveness. Couples can sit at the same table while inhabiting separate universes. Marriage cannot survive on parallel distraction.

7. Financial anxiety and consumerism

Financial fear is real, especially for husbands who bear a strong instinct to provide. Yet anxiety can become an idol. Christ says, "Do not be anxious" and "your heavenly Father knows that you need them all" (Matt 6:25–33). Prudence and hard work remain essential. Yet trust in providence must govern the heart.

8. Undermining fatherhood and motherhood

Contemporary therapeutic culture can sometimes recast all parental authority as oppression. Certainly some parental authority is genuinely abusive and must be named. Yet there is also a broader ideological trend that teaches suspicion toward fathers, mothers, and religious inheritance as such. That erodes the family from within.

9. Isolation from church life

When the Church is no longer experienced as support, sacramental home, and community, couples drift into private struggle. Yet the studies often show that isolation rarely breeds resilience. We are made for communion. The family is a domestic church, though it still needs the larger Church (CCC 1655–1658).

10. Spiritual apathy

One can be Christian and married without living a Christian marriage in any robust sense. If husband and wife do not pray together, seek grace together, and orient their life together toward God, then spiritual apathy will slowly hollow out the covenant.

11. Bitterness and unforgiveness

    Unforgiveness poisons intimacy. Faux apologies only deepen the wound. A real apology names the wrong done. A real act of forgiveness does not deny pain, though it refuses to enthrone resentment. Saint Paul commands, "Be kind to one another, tenderhearted, forgiving one another, as God in Christ forgave you" (Eph 4:32).

12. Third-party intrusions

    From the moment of vows, the couple becomes a new covenantal unit. Parents, siblings, friends, and all others become secondary to the marriage. Emotional confidences that belong properly within the covenant must not be outsourced. Psychological infidelity can become emotional infidelity, then practical infidelity, and eventually physical infidelity. Genesis already gives the structure: "A man leaves his father and mother and cleaves to his wife" (Gen 2:24). That leaving is not symbolic fluff. It is a real reordering of loyalties.

The Book of Tobit and the Defence of Marriage

The Book of Tobit gives us a remarkable icon of spiritual warfare around marriage. Tobias seeks to marry Sarah, though a demon has tormented her and destroyed previous unions before they could be consummated (Tob 3; 6–8). The Archangel Raphael appears, guides Tobias, and reveals that this marriage belongs within God's providence. Tobias and Sarah do not first rush into the marriage chamber in fear or appetite. They pray. Tobias says, "I take this my kinswoman, not because of lust, but with sincerity. Grant that I may find mercy and that we may grow old together" (Tob 8:7, adapted from RSV tradition).

That prayer alone should be written into the hearts of every Christian husband and wife.

Here the pattern is unmistakable. Prayer, angelic assistance, family blessing, divine protection, and chastity of intention become the means by which marriage is defended against the demonic. Tobit teaches that marriages do not flourish in isolation.

They need prayer. They need sacramental grace. They need intercessors. They need the help of heaven.

The Weapons of Warfare

What then is the solution?

First, do not isolate. Seek holy elders, friends, intercessors, and a real church community. Ask people to pray for your marriage. Offer the same for them.

Secondly, pray with each other. Pray for each other. The husband and wife who pray together enter the battle together. The prayer need not always be long. It must, however, be deliberate.

Thirdly, run to the sacraments. Frequent confession. Frequent Eucharist. The Eucharist is "the source and summit of the Christian life" (CCC 1324), and confession restores grace where sin wounds it. The sacramental life is not optional reinforcement. It is the ordinary arsenal of the Christian life.

Fourthly, claim the grace of your sacrament. Matrimony is not a sentimental event in the past. It is an abiding sacramental vocation. The Catechism teaches that the grace proper to marriage is given "to perfect the couple's love and to strengthen their indissoluble unity" (CCC 1641). That grace can and should be invoked.

Fifthly, be deliberately affectionate and intimate. There are few things the devil hates more than a husband and wife who lavish love upon one another. Affection weakens bitterness. Tenderness resists isolation. Intimacy strengthens unity. Charity embodied becomes a shield.

The Church also commends sacramentals, blessings, and consecrated signs, which dispose the faithful to receive grace and cooperate with it (CCC 1667–1670). The nuptial blessing is not decorative language. It is a real ecclesial invocation of grace upon the couple for the battle ahead.

Claim the Grace and Fight Together

Marriage is spiritual warfare. That is not an exaggeration. It is reality.

Yet that does not mean marriage is doomed. It means marriage is important enough to be attacked. It means your union matters enough to hell that hell expends energy against it. It means the covenant you live is a sign of Christ and the Church, and therefore a threat to the kingdom of darkness. Saint Paul says plainly, after speaking of husband and wife, "This is a great mystery, and I mean in reference to Christ and the church" (Eph 5:32).

So spouses must fight accordingly.

They must repent quickly, forgive generously, pray daily, receive the sacraments often, resist isolation, guard their imagination, shut down intrusions, reject counterfeit narratives, and claim the grace of matrimony. They must remember that Christ has already struck the decisive blow. The serpent's head is crushed. The battle still rages, though the outcome is no longer in doubt.

And therefore this prayer is fitting:

Father, I claim the graces of the sacrament of matrimony for all who share in it, and also the graces of baptism, confirmation, and every Eucharist we have received. Deliver our marriages from the works of the evil one. Heal resentment, unforgiveness, wounds, and division. Cover us with angelic protection. Teach us disciplined lives of prayer. Make us loving, affectionate, holy, and courageous. Make us saintly witnesses in a culture of fracture. In Jesus' name. Amen.

Marriage is worth defending because it is worth dying for. Christ has already shown us that. Now we must learn to live it.

Meditation Questions

1. Do I truly believe that my marriage is a site of spiritual warfare, or do I still treat its struggles as merely natural or psychological?
2. Where has Satan most effectively targeted my marriage: fear, distraction, lust, bitterness, isolation, apathy, or something else?
3. If God were to ask me today, "Where are you?" what would be the honest answer regarding my spiritual leadership, fidelity, and prayer?
4. Have I normalised habits, attitudes, or entertainments that quietly undermine my covenant?

5. Am I fighting for my marriage with the weapons God gives, or am I trying to survive without prayer, sacramental grace, and vigilance?
6. Have I let third parties, emotional dependence, digital distraction, or worldly thinking intrude into the sanctuary of my marriage?
7. What one pattern in my marriage most urgently needs to be renounced, confessed, and brought under the lordship of Christ?

Call to Action

Tonight or tomorrow, pray together with your spouse for five minutes and explicitly renounce one spiritual pattern harming your marriage, such as resentment, impurity, fear, distraction, a habitual sin, or unforgiveness. Then ask God together for the grace of your sacrament to overcome it.

Chapter 2

Biblical Wisdom for Husbands

Dying to Self, Living for Christ, & Bringing Heaven into the Home

I presume that many of you men are reading this chapter because, deep down, you believe that marriage is meant to be more than mere survival, more than emotional management, more than a domestic arrangement held together by habit and mutual toleration. Marriage is meant to be a foretaste of heaven. Marriage is meant to be a taste of heaven.

We do not always think of it that way, and yet the Church does. The wisdom of the Church, the witness of Scripture, and the grace of the sacrament all converge on this truth. Marriage is not simply an earthly contract. It is a covenant. It is a sacrament. It is a divine structure through which husband and wife may become saints together and bring the life of heaven into the home.

So let us begin there, with prayer and with Scripture, because this vision can only be grasped if God himself gives it to us.

"Father, I thank you, I praise you, I glorify you for the gift of this wondrous sacrament and covenant that is marriage, which you created as the primordial covenant, the structure through which man and woman were meant to live together. Even without civil law, even without a justice of the peace, you are the designer of marriage and the family. Pierce our hearts so that we may begin to see that our marriages are really meant to be heaven on earth. Let this be an hour of conversion, a breakthrough, so that whatever is holding us back from a heavenly marriage may be laid at the foot of the cross. Mary, our Blessed Mother, and Joseph, pray for us. Amen."

The Premise: Heaven Through Suffering

The foundational text for this chapter is Romans 8:17. Saint Paul is speaking of our adoption as children of God. He says, "For all who are led by the Spirit of God are sons of God" (Rom 8:14). He then declares that we have received "the Spirit of sonship" by whom we cry, "Abba! Father!" (Rom 8:15). Everything sounds glorious. Then Paul reaches his conclusion: "And if children, then heirs, heirs of God and fellow heirs with Christ, provided we suffer with him in order that we may also be glorified with him" (Rom 8:17).

If Paul had stopped just before that final clause, it would have been a wonderfully comforting passage. Instead he tells us plainly that glory comes through suffering. Heaven comes through the cross.

That is where many people go wrong in their understanding of marriage. No one told us that marriage was meant to be death to self. No one told us that marriage would require crucifixion. No one told many men growing up that to be a husband was to become, in a real sense, a dying man. Yet that is exactly what Christian marriage requires. If Romans 8:17 is true, then the way to glory is the way of suffering with Christ. Marriage, if it is to become heavenly, must therefore become cruciform.

That is especially true for men. We are not merely warriors, though the image has its uses. We are meant to be priests, prophets, and kings within the household. In Scripture, the priest, the prophet, and the king are those who die to themselves in service. The husband is called to a headship that is sacrificial, not self-serving. The husband's authority is moral only if it is crucified.

This is why Ephesians 5 is so often misunderstood. Much attention is given to the line, "Wives, be subject to your husbands, as to the Lord" (Eph 5:22). Yet the real burden of the passage falls with devastating seriousness on the husband: "Husbands, love your wives, as Christ loved the church and gave himself up for her" (Eph 5:25). Christ loved the Church by dying for her. He gave himself up for her. He sanctified her. He washed her "by the washing of water with the word" (Eph 5:26).

So yes, one can say to a wife, "Trust your husband's spiritual leadership," though only on one condition: that he is infinitely more submitted to Christ than he expects her to be to him. The husband's authority is never an independent power. It is always a stewardship under Christ. In that sense, men have the harder burden. The wife is called to trust. The husband is called to become trustworthy by grace, sacrifice, prayer, discipline, and self-forgetfulness.

And yet this is precisely where heaven begins.

The Lie of the Culture About Marriage

I know this sounds painful, especially to men. Yet I must speak candidly. Much of the counsel many men received about marriage was poisoned from the beginning. The only real advice I received from my father about marriage was this: "Whatever you do, don't get married." That was not merely his private bitterness. It echoed the message of the secular culture. Marriage was portrayed as entrapment, as loss, as the death of personal freedom, as a burden imposed on masculine life.

Why does the culture speak that way? Because marriage is an assault on selfishness. The culture does not mind romance, desire, pleasure, companionship, or cohabitation so long as the self remains enthroned. What it resists is covenant, because covenant demands surrender. Covenant says that my life is no longer merely my own.

And that is why marriage becomes a path toward heaven. If Romans 8:17 is to be taken seriously, then glory comes only if we suffer with Christ. In lesser terms, one might say that we must pass through a kind of hell before heaven is ours. That can happen now through crucifixion of self, or later through judgment. Those are the options laid before us. We may cling to selfishness now and lose heaven later, or we may die to selfishness now and begin to taste heaven already.

This is the entire biblical pattern. Resurrection comes through crucifixion. Glory comes through self-emptying. Love comes through sacrifice. Marriage belongs fully to that pattern.

Baptism, Spiritual Marriage, and the Wedding Feast of the Lamb

The heavenly nature of marriage becomes even clearer when we turn to Revelation 19. There Saint John hears the heavenly multitude crying, "Hallelujah! For the Lord our God the Almighty reigns" (Rev 19:6). Then comes the astonishing proclamation: "Let us rejoice and exult and give him the glory, for the marriage of the Lamb has come, and his Bride has made herself ready" (Rev 19:7). The Bride is clothed "with fine linen, bright and pure" (Rev 19:8).

This is not ornamental imagery. It is the unveiling of the destiny of the Church. Christ is the Bridegroom. The Church is the Bride. Heaven is described as a wedding feast.

This means that every baptised Christian already lives within a nuptial mystery. In baptism we are joined to Christ and incorporated into his Bride, the Church. In that sense, every baptised person participates in a kind of spiritual marriage. This does not erase the distinction between sacramental Matrimony and the universal vocation of the baptised. It means rather that marriage is not a peripheral image in Christian life. It is a primary spiritual structure. The covenant between Christ and the Church is the pattern. Earthly Christian marriage becomes one of its most luminous expressions.

The Catechism teaches that the whole Christian life bears the mark of "the spousal love of Christ and the Church," and that Baptism is already an entry into this nuptial mystery (CCC 1617). Earthly marriage, therefore, is never merely natural. In Christ it is elevated and taken up into divine love (CCC 1639). That is why marriage can become heaven on earth. It participates in the very mystery toward which all history is moving.

Small Acts, Hidden Holiness, and the Sanctification of the Household

What does this mean practically?

It means that all the little acts of fidelity in marriage are not merely chores, tasks, and annoyances. They are caught up into sanctification. When Saint Paul says that Christ sanctifies the Church "by the washing of water with the word" (Eph 5:26), he is speaking first of Christ. Yet he is also giving husbands an image by which to understand their own vocation. The husband's faithfulness, sacrifice, provision, tenderness, and service all become instruments through which his wife and children are sanctified. He may never see the full effect of this in earthly life. Yet grace is at work in the hidden things.

I have three children. I am blessed beyond measure. The ordinary things of family life, bathing children, changing diapers, taking out the rubbish, cleaning, fixing, carrying, staying faithful in work, showing up tired, remaining patient, these things do not look mystical. Yet in the economy of grace they participate in the sanctification of the household. A husband who takes out the rubbish in fidelity to his vocation may never say, "This is making my bride a saint," though in the mystery of the sacrament, such acts truly do contribute to holiness.

That is what many men miss. We think retreats, prayer, talks, and spiritual exhortation are somehow disconnected from masculine desire and domestic life. Meanwhile, the hidden duties of the home are precisely the field in which our sanctification unfolds. The domestic life is not beneath the spiritual life. It is one of its chief theatres.

The Catechism teaches that the grace of Matrimony "is intended to perfect the couple's love and to strengthen their indissoluble unity" (CCC 1641). This means that ordinary acts of covenantal fidelity really do become channels of grace. The family home is therefore rightly called the domestic church (CCC 1655–1658). What happens there matters eternally.

Men, Lead the Charge

This is why I keep returning to the men.

In a later chapter I would unpack Genesis 3 at greater length, though the essential point is this. Satan comes after Eve. Adam is right there. The text says that after she took the fruit, "she also gave some to her husband who was with her, and he ate" (Gen 3:6). Adam stood there and did nothing. He failed to protect. He failed to intervene. He failed to speak. He failed to shepherd.

That pattern continues in countless marriages. Think of the areas of strife, fear, anxiety, and confusion that can overtake a wife when her interior world is not being met with spiritual leadership. I have seen this in my own marriage. My wife, staying home with children, receiving a constant bombardment of cultural narratives, political panic, social fear, and moral instability, could easily become anxious about the world, about our family, about the future, about our children. I realised at one point that though I was going on the radio daily speaking about the sovereignty of God, coming home, playing with the children, and trying to love my wife well, I was failing in one decisive area: I was not speaking the truths of God directly enough into her life.

I was not assuring her concretely that God is Lord not only of the culture, not only of the state, not only of the nation, though of our house, our marriage, our children, and our daily bread. That omission in me contributed to unrest in her. Once I saw it, I had to repent and bring it before the Lord.

This is what I mean when I say to men: love your bride enough to love Jesus more than her first. It is only by loving Christ first that you will love her rightly. If you put her first in the place where only Christ belongs, you will crush her under a burden she was never meant to bear. If you love Christ first, then you will receive from him the grace, truth, courage, and selflessness by which you may love her as she deserves.

That is the only way the household becomes heavenly.

A Happy Marriage in a Broken World

I was never given a model of a happy marriage. I did not grow up believing marriage could be joyful. And yet I can say now, with gratitude to God, that I have the happiest marriage I could have imagined.

My bride is my best friend after Jesus. I miss her when I am away. I am grateful when I am near her. This is not because I am naturally good at marriage. It is because the love of God has entered our covenant and is slowly making us holy.

Christ at the centre changes everything. The more I pour my heart out for Christ, the better husband I become. The more I take my eyes off Christ, the poorer a husband I become. She is the first to let me know this. And that is one of God's mercies.

My wife and I also made an implicit commitment which, in truth, is already written into the meaning of the vows: we will not allow the other to fall into mortal sin. We share everything. We hide nothing. We are accountable to one another. Confession is a regular part of my life, often once a week or every two weeks, and every time I return from the sacrament, I can see more clearly the small ways in which I have failed her, ways that easily accumulate into larger wounds if left unexamined. The sacrament restores sight. It teaches me again that marriage is heaven on earth only because it is constantly being rescued from hell by grace.

This is why Satan hates it. He attacks the bride first because he wants the husband and the family after that. Destroy marriage, and one destabilises the family. Destroy the family, and one weakens the Church. Destroy the Church, and society decays. There is nothing original about the strategy. It is old, methodical, and devastating.

Which is why your marriage matters so much more than you think. Your covenant is not merely private happiness. It is one of the greatest acts of resistance against a culture of fragmentation.

The Groom in Black

There is a simple story that makes this point with humour. A young boy watches a bride being escorted down the aisle in her beautiful white gown. He asks his mother, "Why is she wearing white on her wedding day?" The mother replies, "Because it is the happiest day of her life." The boy then looks at the groom standing at the altar dressed in black and asks, "Then why is he wearing black?"

It is funny because it reveals something real. The bride's white signifies joy. The groom's black, one might say, signifies funeral attire. On that day, he begins to die. Marcus Peter no longer lives for Marcus Peter. That is what the husband's vows mean if he lives them worthily. From that moment on, his authority within the covenant becomes a stewardship of selflessness. He cannot think of himself first.

This is where modern culture goes astray. Fulton Sheen observed with great brilliance that the modern man and woman enter marriage seeking from the other what only God can provide, namely final fulfilment. Their disappointment then becomes one of the causes of marital collapse. The spouse was never meant to bear that burden.

Your bride is not here on earth to fulfil all your desires and needs. Your husband is not here to anticipate every preference, every mood, every psychological shift, every internal hunger. Human beings change constantly. Our tastes change. Our habits change. Our struggles change. Our bodies change. If I cannot keep pace even with my own inner changes, how can I demand that my spouse fulfil them all?

That is why marriage fails when it begins in selfishness. We go into it with the self at the centre, and then we wonder why disappointment breeds resentment. Yet love is not that. Love is not a feeling, whatever the songs may say. Love is the daily willing of the good of the other over the self. In that sense, one does not simply "fall out of love." Love grows as it is chosen.

I can say with truth that after seven years, I love my bride more now than I did on the day we were married. And if I continue choosing rightly, I will love her more tomorrow than I do today. That is the real increase of love.

Generativity, Receptivity, and the Life of Heaven in the Home

There is also a profound theological meaning in the very structure of male and female.

The husband's gift is, in part, generative. He is called to receive from God and pour outward in sacrificial love. The wife's gift is, in part, receptive, though not passive. Her receptivity is a strength, a fruitfulness, a gestating power. Even in the biological order, human beings do not merely reproduce in the way animals do. We procreate with God. We cooperate in the generation of immortal souls. The husband gives, the wife receives, and from that one-flesh union comes life that neither could produce alone.

When my wife and I look at our children, we are looking at the embodied fruit of covenantal love. Our love now has arms and legs and names and personalities. It laughs, cries, runs, and prays. That is astounding. God gave woman the power to receive a gift of love and bring it to fruition in life.

This also has a spiritual analogue in the home. The more selfless I become, the more I create safety for my wife to pour forth her own love fruitfully. The holier and more prayerful I become, the more space is made for her to flourish as a saint. The husband's spiritual leadership is not control. It is the creation of a climate in which heaven can breathe.

This is why men must take up the charge. Let your bride and your children see you pray. Let them hear you speak the word of God. Read Scripture aloud in the home. Even one chapter a day can begin to alter the atmosphere of a household. Pour into your bride the word of God, and you will find that as you die to yourself, heaven displaces the hell you have been living.

This does not mean there will be no suffering. My own marriage has had hard years and sharp trials. Yet I would not trade this life for anything because even through suffering, it has become happy in a deeply heavenly way.

Heaven Can Be Born in the Family

Many of those hearing this are parents of adult children and grandparents of grandchildren. The principle remains the same. Be visible in love. Be tender. Be prayerful. Be affectionate. Let the children and grandchildren see the reality of holy marriage. The love that flows from husband to wife and wife to husband is not meant to stop with the couple. It spills outward into generations. It forms a pattern, a memory, a witness, a climate, and in many cases a healing of inherited wounds.

Heaven can be born in a family. That is not sentimentality. It is a sacramental reality. The Church teaches that Christian spouses have their own gifts among the People of God and that by their vocation they build up the Body of Christ (CCC 1641–1642). The holy marriage of one generation can become the stabilising grace of the next.

And that is why the prayer at the end must be bold.

"Father, see in the hands of these husbands the tender hands of their brides. Renew in them the nuptial blessing they received on the day of their marriage. You consecrated them. You empowered them. You gave them grace that no merely human arrangement can offer. Let that grace heal what is broken, soften what is stubborn, uproot resentment, and restore what has grown cold. Whatever blocks these marriages from being heavenly right now, take it, O Lord. Be the lover of their souls. Let their marriages sing your praise even unto death. Bless also their children and grandchildren, that their yes may become a grace for generations."

Be Romantic, Become Holy

Marriage is meant to be heaven on earth. It is meant to be a foretaste of the wedding feast of the Lamb. That does not mean it is effortless. It means it is cruciform. It means that heaven enters the home through sacrifice, prayer, tenderness, confession, fidelity, and grace.

So then, brothers, be a little more romantic with your bride today. Not as sentimentality. Not as manipulation. Not as theatre. Do it because affection is holy. A hand held with love, an arm placed gently around her, a kiss on the forehead, a word of tenderness, a passage of Scripture read aloud, a hidden act of service, these are not trivialities. In the mystery of the sacrament, they are making you a saint and making her a saint.

Marriage is not merely the place where two people try to be happy. It is the place where two people help one another into heaven.

Meditation Questions

1. Do I really believe that marriage is meant to be a foretaste of heaven, or have I reduced it to duty, routine, or survival?
2. In what concrete ways am I still resisting death to self within my marriage?

3. Have I wrongly expected my spouse to fulfil desires and needs that only God can rightly satisfy?
4. How is Christ presently calling me to become more self-giving, more prayerful, and more faithful in my vocation?
5. Are the ordinary duties of my married and family life becoming channels of sanctification, or am I treating them as interruptions?
6. What do my children, grandchildren, or others actually learn about marriage by watching me live mine?
7. Where do I most need heaven to break into my home right now: speech, affection, trust, prayer, forgiveness, leadership, or peace?

Call to Action

For the next seven days, do one deliberate act of tender self-gift for your spouse each day without announcing it, and end each evening by thanking God for one way your marriage has been a sign of grace.

Chapter 3

Biblical Wisdom for Wives

Woman as Helpmate, Remedy, and Strength in the Covenant

The title of this chapter is Satan's 12 Attacks on Wives, and it bears a subtitle that may initially unsettle some women: the fall of woman. Ladies, there is every chance you may not like the opening portion of this chapter. Yet stay with me, because it ends where it ought to end, namely in showing how women are, in the providence of God, a remedy within marriage, and how wives are called to draw forth the virtue to which their husbands have been summoned.

Throughout most of my writings and talks, I have been exhaustive on men, and perhaps rather hard on men, because I grew up in circumstances where men did not rise up. Therefore I had to learn how to be a man largely on my own, and how to be a husband and father through struggle, prayer, discipline, and grace. This particular chapter is usually the content of a talk given by my bride, and I am borrowing heavily from her wisdom. My own bearing here is covenant theology. Her expertise is biblical theology of the body. So I am sharing with you some of what she would have said, and I will also share a little of her wisdom near the end.

The Woman as God's Help in the Household

I want to begin with a concept that comes directly from the Catechism of the Catholic Church. Holy Mother Church exhorts women to understand that their role as wives is indeed deeply receptive. The wife receives the life, the initiative, and the generativity of her husband, and then nurtures that gift into a life-giving force that overflows into the household, into the children, into culture, and into society. That is completely true.

At the same time, if you have read Fulton Sheen's *Three to Get Married*, then you know that he makes the point very clearly that as go the women, so goes the culture. He adds a necessary caveat. As go the men, so go the women. In other words, the rise of unvirtuous women is in significant part bound up with the rise of unvirtuous men. That is worth remembering, especially since so much social analysis today is stripped of reciprocity and covenantal mutuality.

Still, I want first to present this truth. If men are failing to rise, or if men are struggling to rise, then part of the wife's role in complementarity is that God has given her a tender grace by which she can call virtue out of her husband. She does this differently from a man. She is not meant to become his rival, his accuser, or his drill sergeant. She is not meant to scream, to shame, or to bludgeon him with Bible verses. Rather, in feminine tenderness she can say, "I need this of you. I need you to rise in this way because I need to be this, and I cannot do this without you."

That, in fact, reveals the pillar God calls her to be in the marriage. The husband is indeed meant to uphold his wife, to be her strength, her protector, and her provider. Yet that headship exists so that she may have the space to flourish as woman, and to call forth virtue in the household. Marriage, then, is never merely one-directional. It is reciprocal, though never interchangeable.

The Catechism states, "Holy Scripture affirms that man and woman were created for one another: 'It is not good that the man should be alone.' The woman, 'flesh of his flesh,' his equal, his nearest in all things, is given to him by God as a 'helpmate'; she thus represents God from whom comes our help" (CCC 1605, citing Gen 2:18–25). That is an astonishing claim. She "represents God from whom comes our help."

This corresponds to the language of Genesis. "Then the Lord God said, 'It is not good that the man should be alone; I will make him a helper fit for him'" (Gen 2:18). The Hebrew expression behind this, often discussed as *ezer kenegdo*, does not signify a mere assistant or domestic subordinate. In Scripture, ezer frequently refers to God himself as helper. "God is our refuge and strength, a very present help in trouble" (Ps 46:1). Moses blesses Israel by saying, "There is none like God, O Jeshurun, who rides through the heavens to your help" (Deut 33:26). Therefore the biblical language itself rules out every cheap caricature of the wife as spiritually secondary. She is given as a help so profound that Scripture uses God-language to illuminate her role.

Ladies, if no one has ever told you this before, then hear it clearly. You are called, in a unique domestic sense, to manifest something of the presence of God within the household. That does not make you divine. It means that in the economy of marriage your vocation has a theological depth greater than the modern world can fathom.

Marriage as a Participation in Trinitarian Life

If men are called to image the fatherhood of God through originative love, providence, protection, and sacrificial initiative, then the wife, in receiving and reciprocating that love, images something profoundly analogous to the Son's eternal receptivity and self-giving toward the Father. The Son eternally receives all from the Father and eternally returns all in love. That love is so perfect, so fruitful, so total, that the Church speaks of the Holy Spirit as proceeding from the Father and the Son. Marriage, in its creaturely and sacramental way, reflects this mystery.

Saint John Paul II taught that in marital consent each spouse gives himself or herself irreversibly to the other, and that this mutual self-gift reveals "the spousal meaning of the body" and the very structure of personal communion. As he wrote, "By its very nature, the institution of marriage and married love is ordered to the procreation and education of the offspring and it is in them that it finds its crowning glory" (Gaudium et Spes, 48; cf. Familiaris Consortio, 11–14). The Catechism likewise teaches that conjugal love "involves a totality, in which all the elements of the person enter" (CCC 1643).

That is why marriage and family uniquely mirror the Trinitarian life. No other vocation does this in the same way. Other vocations mirror divine realities with their own splendour. Yet the family is a distinct icon. Husband, wife, and child reveal in creaturely form a communion of persons marked by love, fruitfulness, and covenant.

I often explain this by saying that I am not merely the father of several children. Rather, I am a father many times over. The family is composed, as it were, of repeated communions between husband, wife, and each child. The language is imperfect, of course, because every analogy with the Trinity limps. Yet the point remains. Each child extends and deepens the family's participation in a life of communion. The family thus becomes a living school of self-gift, of love that receives, returns, protects, nourishes, and sanctifies.

The Long History of Failure in Salvation History

Earlier in the week I said that the history of salvation can in one sense be summed up by the line: a husband failed his bride. Adam failed Eve. Israel's kings failed the covenant people. Fathers failed households. Shepherds failed the flock. That is true.

Yet there is a footnote which is not really a footnote. At times, a bride also failed to rise to her call. I say this carefully and humbly, because this point usually comes more naturally from my wife than from me. Still, Scripture gives us patterns that are meant for our instruction. Saint Paul says, "Whatever was written in former days was written for our instruction" (Rom 15:4). So let us be instructed.

Women are meant, in receptivity, to be strong. I have lost count of the times my bride has been a blindside mirror in my spiritual life, calling my attention to areas I was not seeing. Men are often like racehorses with blinders. We see the finish line. We see the objective. We see the distant threat. We see the future target. We are made for achievement, pursuit, protection, and fight. That is part of male nature, both biologically and theologically. Yet because of that, we can miss the near things, the proximate wounds, the subtle tensions, the domestic fractures.

Women often see more of what is near. Their hearts hold the closer things closer. There is a reason a wife can find the ketchup in the refrigerator when the husband cannot, even while he is staring directly at it. Men often see through the trees to the deer. Women often see the things right in front of the family's soul.

That is part of what people today have called the feminine genius. Saint John Paul II spoke of this "particular sensitivity" which belongs to woman and which enables her to perceive the person with a unique attentiveness (Mulieris Dignitatem, 18, 30). That attentiveness is not a weakness. It is a gift ordered to love, to realism, to tenderness, and to sanctification.

Eve and the Silent Husband

We begin with Eve. In Genesis 3, Adam stands there in silence while Eve is tempted. The serpent addresses the woman, and the man who should have guarded, intervened, and protected remains passive. The text says that after she took the fruit, "she also gave some to her husband, and he ate" (Gen 3:6). He is there. He is silent. He is absent in the very place where he is physically present.

That much I have emphasised elsewhere. Yet there is another dimension. If Eve is the beloved wife of Adam, then when a strange and malignant voice begins to seduce, distort, and pull her away from truth, she ought to turn toward her husband and say, in essence, "Protect me. Speak. Rise. Guard this covenant." The temptation against Eve remains the temptation against women today. The serpent's strategies are not creative. He repeats the same old patterns.

The culture now tells women, "Your husband must not be your primary confidant. Do not turn to him first. Seek elsewhere. Find another emotional centre." As soon as a third party is inserted into the sanctuary of husband and wife, that third voice often validates every grievance, magnifies every suspicion, and gradually feeds strife into the marriage. Scripture says, "Therefore a man leaves his father and his mother and cleaves to his wife, and they become one flesh" (Gen 2:24). Christ himself repeats this and adds, "What therefore God has joined together, let no man put asunder" (Matt 19:6). The unity of marriage must therefore be guarded, especially in speech, counsel, and emotional dependence.

A wife has real power to call a husband into his office. If she says with tenderness and truth, "I need you to protect me," there are very few husbands who will remain inert. A man who has forgotten his strength can sometimes remember it again when his bride calls him to it.

Noah, Abraham, Moses, and David

The story of Noah in Genesis 9 is strange and disturbing. After the flood he plants a vineyard, drinks of the wine, and lies exposed in his tent. The traditional English rendering says that Ham "saw the nakedness of his father" (Gen 9:22). Yet the wider biblical usage, especially illuminated by Leviticus 18, suggests that "uncovering nakedness" can indicate sexual violation involving the father's wife. Leviticus says, "You shall not uncover the nakedness of your father's wife; it is your father's nakedness" (Lev 18:8). Within an ancient Near Eastern context, to seize the king's wife was a way of laying claim to his authority and his household. Later, Absalom does precisely this in rebellion against David (2 Sam 16:21–22).

The point here is not to indulge speculative novelty. The point is that sin against covenant order attacks both headship and sanctity. Noah fails through intemperance. Disorder enters the household. Shame, violation, and rupture follow. The covenant head stumbles, and the household reels.

Then Abraham. In Genesis 12 he allows Sarai to be taken into Pharaoh's house through fear. In Genesis 20 he repeats the pattern with Abimelech. In Genesis 16, through the counsel of Sarai, Hagar is introduced into the household in a way that fractures covenant peace. Abraham fails in courage and trust. Sarah fails in places to resist, to object, or to hold the line of the promise. In all of this, God remains faithful, because the covenant finally rests on divine fidelity rather than human steadiness. Yet these narratives still teach us.

Moses too gives us strange scenes. In Exodus 4 there is the crisis involving circumcision, where Zipporah intervenes decisively to ward off judgment (Exod 4:24–26). There she does act. There she perceives. There she moves. That very text proves the broader principle. A wife can, at a critical point, become the instrument through which disorder is checked and covenant obligation is remembered. Later, Moses also falls through anger and self-reference, especially at Meribah, where he says, "Shall we bring forth water for you out of this rock?" (Num 20:10), and judgment follows.

David gives us several patterns. Bathsheba enters the narrative through David's abuse of royal power (2 Sam 11). Michal, in 2 Samuel 6, sees David dancing before the ark and despises him in her heart. Her contempt is directed at the very place where his zeal for the Lord is being expressed. The wife who ceases to see the husband's heart before God easily grows cold toward the husband himself.

The point in all these stories is not to stack blame against women. It is to show that covenant breakdown often involves failure on both sides. Husband and wife are bound together in mutual sanctification or mutual collapse. That is why the sacrament matters so much.

The Call to Mutual Sanctification

The remedy is fidelity to God on both sides. Prudence, justice, temperance, and fortitude are required of husband and wife alike. We men need our brides to be saints. Ladies, we need you to be saints for our sake. We are willing to fight for you. We want to fight for you. We want to lay down our lives for you, because Saint Paul commands husbands, "Love your wives, as Christ loved the church and gave himself up for her" (Eph 5:25). Yet we cannot fight this battle alone, and God never intended us to.

The wife is more than a passive helpmate. She is meant to stand in battle beside her husband. This is why family prayer matters. Get on your knees together. Pray the rosary together. Go to confession regularly. Receive the Eucharist frequently. The Catechism teaches that the Eucharist is "the source and summit of the Christian life" (CCC 1324), and marriage cannot flourish while severed from its sacramental source. Likewise, the grace of Penance restores what sin wounds. Vatican II teaches that the sacraments "confer the grace that they signify" and dispose the faithful to worship God rightly (Sacrosanctum Concilium, 59).

If one spouse has delayed Confirmation, seek it. Receive all the sacramental helps the Church offers. Grace does not replace nature, yet it heals, elevates, strengthens, and sends nature on mission. In marriage that mission is holiness.

Saint John Paul II wrote, "Christian marriage, like each sacrament, 'whose purpose is to sanctify people, to build up the Body of Christ, and, finally, to give worship to God,' is in itself a liturgical action glorifying God in Jesus Christ and in the Church" (Familiaris Consortio, 56). Marriage is therefore not merely a private arrangement. It is a sacramental mission.

The Wife's Vow and the Gift of the Person

John Paul II speaks magnificently of marriage as an irrevocable gift of person to person. "By its very nature, the gift of the person must be lasting and irrevocable," and "the indissolubility of marriage flows in the very first place from the essence of that gift" (Love and Responsibility; cf. Familiaris Consortio, 11). In the marriage rite the bride says, "I take you as my husband. I promise to be true to you in good times and in bad, in sickness and in health. I will love you and honour you all the days of my life." The husband says the same.

That vow includes more than companionship. It includes a solemn commitment to the other's sanctification. My bride and I have made it explicit between us that we will never allow the other to fall into mortal sin if we can help it. We hold one another accountable to heaven.

This ministry of mine would be nothing without my wife. We read Scripture together. We discuss theology together. She brings her immersion in the theology of the body, the feminine perspective, and the spiritual insight of a wife and mother. I bring covenant theology, Ratzinger, Aquinas, biblical structure, and theological synthesis. She enlightens me in ways I cannot fully describe because I need her. Every talk I have given, every exhortation, every word that has borne fruit in public, has also been shaped in private through the love, wisdom, sacrifice, and fidelity of my bride.

Twelve Ways Satan Attacks Wives

What follows is a list, largely distilled from the wisdom of my wife, of ways Satan often draws women away from their vocation within marriage.

1. Suspicion

> The mind can become easily suspicious when another voice enters and tempts it. Something done innocently by the husband is interpreted as malice. Suspicion poisons peace.

2. Comparison and Discontent

A woman compares her husband to caricatures of masculinity, to other men, to public personas, to polished fragments of other marriages. Yet God did not give her every husband. God gave her her husband. Her task is to love that husband and call forth the good in that husband.

3. Contempt

The feminine heart is deep, and when it is wounded and unforgiveness is left untreated, contempt can grow. The husband may think a conflict has ended while the wound remains alive in the wife's interior world. This requires healing, prayer, and mercy. Saint Paul says, "Let all bitterness and wrath and anger and clamor and slander be put away from you" (Eph 4:31).

4. Recruiting Allies Against Him

The culture teaches women to seek emotional solidarity outside the marriage in ways that steadily turn into resentment toward husbands. This is spiritually dangerous. It violates the covenantal intimacy of marriage.

5. Unresolved Wounds Becoming a Lens

When hurts are never properly healed, they become the interpretive lens through which the husband is seen. His every action is read through old pain.

6. Control Masked as Virtue

A wife, having been hurt repeatedly, can begin to micromanage the husband under the appearance of moral concern. Then the husband often checks out internally. This cycle becomes destructive.

7. Sexual Resentment

Where emotional safety collapses, intimacy can become weaponised or withdrawn. Yet physical and emotional intimacy, rightly ordered, are meant by God to heal and deepen communion. Saint Paul teaches spouses not to deprive one another except for a time devoted to prayer, and then to come together again (1 Cor 7:3–5).

8. Endless Critique and Perfectionism

The accumulation of small resentments can produce a critical worldview in which the husband can do little right.

9. Distortion of Respect

Men often read disrespect as a statement that they are unloved. Women often read disregard for their interiority as a statement that they are unloved. Both wounds are real. Saint Paul therefore says, "Let each one of you love his wife as himself, and let the wife see that she respects her husband" (Eph 5:33).

10. Spiritual Counterfeit

Piety without charity. Church activity becomes a refuge from marital pain rather than a place from which grace is brought back into the marriage.

11. Catastrophising and Hopeless Narratives

"He will never change." "This is beyond repair." "There is no point." Such narratives choke grace and kill perseverance.

12. Isolation Inside the Home

The mother and children become an emotional island within the home, while the father becomes a tolerated outsider. This fractures the domestic church. The family is not meant to become parallel relational worlds under one roof.

All of these patterns need grace, vigilance, repentance, tenderness, and spiritual discipline.

Presence, Tenderness, and the Domestic Covenant

A husband must invest his presence in the home. Work matters. Provision matters. Yet presence matters too. My own workdays are long, often ten to twelve hours, and yet when I clock off, I must become fully present. I must play with my son. I must hold my daughters. I must enter the life of the home.

I have a rule. When I get home and the children run to greet me, I stop them and say, "Mama gets the first kiss." I go to my bride first because I want my children to see that daddy loves mommy. I want them to know that this covenant is first, and that from its strength their own lives receive peace.

At the end of the day, my wife and I share what we call our "most endearing moment." We name some little thing the other did that day which made us feel loved. Time and again I think the grand gesture will be what impressed her, yet she often tells me that what moved her most was seeing me play with one of the children, or holding a child on my lap, or entering their little world. The things men and women instinctively register as most endearing are often different. That is exactly why women must tell men what reaches their hearts. In doing so, they help call forth the husband they long for.

A Wife's First Priorities

My bride once shared this exhortation with women. She said that Satan often distracts women through practical things, through the home, through children, through cooking, through caring for others, through the thousand demands of daily life. All of those things matter. All of them can be privileges. Yet at the end of the day, Christ must come first, and then the marriage must be guarded with deliberate priority.

That accords with Catholic teaching. The Second Vatican Council teaches that spouses "help one another to attain holiness in their married life and in welcoming and educating their children" (Lumen Gentium, 11). The family is a "domestic church." The Catechism echoes this, saying, "The Christian home is the place where children receive the first proclamation of the faith. For this reason the family home is rightly called 'the domestic church'" (CCC 1666).

Yet a domestic church cannot flourish if husband and wife stop tending the altar of their own covenant. The children matter profoundly, though the marriage remains foundational. To place children functionally above the sacrament of marriage is to weaken the very structure on which their flourishing depends.

Final Exhortation to Wives

Ladies, express to your husbands the vulnerability of your heart. Tell him how much you need him. Tell him how much you want him. Tell him that you are committed to his sanctity. Tell him that you will respect him, encourage him, and call him to become the man God wants him to be. That is not domination. That is covenantal cooperation with grace.

The Blessed Virgin Mary gives us the supreme model of receptivity joined to strength. The Church calls her the "New Eve" because by her obedience she untied the knot of Eve's disobedience (CCC 411; cf.

St Irenaeus, Against Heresies 3.22.4). She was full of grace, yet she still lived in reverence, humility, and covenant fidelity. At Cana she sees what others miss. She perceives need. She intercedes. She directs the servants, "Do whatever he tells you" (John 2:5). There is the feminine vocation in miniature: attentive perception, tender intercession, and unwavering orientation toward Christ.

Marriage is not happiness without suffering. It is a sanctified communion that learns to move through suffering with grace. It is the place where a wife can choose respect even when her husband fails, and where a husband can choose tenderness, selflessness, and sacrifice even when wounded. It is the place where two sinners are slowly made holy together.

So then, let every wife ask for the grace to reopen what resentment has closed, to forgive what memory keeps replaying, and to stand beside her husband in battle. Let every husband ask for the grace to rise, protect, lead, repent, and love sacrificially. Let both remember that they are meant, by the grace of the sacrament, to become saints together.

For "love bears all things, believes all things, hopes all things, endures all things" (1 Cor 13:7). And the grace of Christ does not merely decorate marriage from the outside. It enters it, heals it, and raises it into a participation in divine love.

May every Christian marriage become what it was always meant to be: a living covenant, a domestic church, a school of holiness, and a radiant witness to the love of Christ and his Church.

Meditation Questions

1. In what ways have I misunderstood my wife's role as "helper" and failed to see its biblical and theological dignity?
2. Have I treated complementarity as competition, or have I received it as God's design for mutual sanctification?
3. Where in my marriage have I failed to call forth virtue in my spouse with tenderness, truth, and humility?
4. Have I allowed resentment, contempt, suspicion, or comparison to distort the way I see my spouse?
5. Do I truly believe that my spouse is part of God's ordinary means of making me holy?

6. In moments of temptation, discouragement, or confusion, do I turn first toward my spouse in covenantal trust, or away into isolation and third-party dependence?
7. What concrete patterns in my marriage need healing so that we may better reflect the life-giving communion God intended from the beginning?

Call to Action

Set aside 20 minutes this week for an honest conversation with your spouse in which each of you answers this question aloud: "How can I better help you become a saint?" Then write down one concrete change each of you will begin immediately. Start praying with each other daily. An example of a very small prayer: "Father, please bless your marriage and journey to sainthood together. Amen."

Chapter 4

Satan's Attack on Marital Intimacy

Satan's Attack on Marital Intimacy

I am about to teach on something that many of you have lived far longer than I have. If I am writing to couples who have been married ten years, twenty years, thirty years, even longer, then I am conscious that I am addressing people with more lived wisdom than I possess. I have been married seven years at the time of this writing, and many of you have gone much farther down this road than I have. So I begin with humility, with prayer, and with the intercession of Our Lady, because this chapter concerns something sacred, misunderstood, and very often attacked.

This chapter is about the grace of marriage, with a subtitle that may initially strike some as startling: Satan's attack on Marital Intimacy. If you have never thought of your marital intimacy in those categories, then I hope what follows will help you begin to do so.

I also want to encourage you to break out of any secular mentality by which you have been taught to think about intimacy as husband and wife. This will not be explicit. It will, however, be deeply biblical, deeply theological, and resolutely Catholic. My desire is to give you something of God's own view of the union between bride and bridegroom.

In earlier chapters, I unpacked the fall narrative in Genesis 3, how Satan attacked Eve and how Adam failed in his vocation. Here I want to continue that same conversation, though from a different angle. Yesterday the focus was the temptation itself. Today the focus is what followed from it, and what that means for marriage, intimacy, holiness, and spiritual warfare.

The Curse after the Fall & What it Actually Means

After Adam and Eve eat of the fruit, the Lord speaks judgment into the wreckage of the fall. To the woman he says, "I will greatly multiply your pain in childbearing; in pain you shall bring forth children, yet your desire shall be for your husband, and he shall rule over you" (Gen 3:16). To the man he says,

"Cursed is the ground because of you; in toil you shall eat of it all the days of your life" (Gen 3:17). Then the Lord continues: "Thorns and thistles it shall bring forth to you; and you shall eat the plants of the field. In the sweat of your face you shall eat bread till you return to the ground" (Gen 3:18–19).

We need to ask a careful question here. What exactly is being cursed?

To answer that, we must go back to the beginning. When man and woman were first created, they were told, "Be fruitful and multiply, and fill the earth and subdue it" (Gen 1:28). That command is not a crude biological instruction. It is a revelation of divine design. God had already built into the original, unfallen order the intimacy of husband and wife and the fruitfulness of children. In other words, marital union was never a later concession to sin, nor a mere practical arrangement for companionship, nor merely a biological mechanism for reproduction. It belonged to the original goodness of creation.

The Catechism teaches that conjugal love is "caught up into divine love" (CCC 1639). It also teaches that "the acts in marriage by which the intimate and chaste union of the spouses takes place are noble and honorable" (CCC 2362, quoting Gaudium et Spes, 49). That is a remarkable claim. Marital intimacy is not something spiritually neutral that sits beside the sacrament of marriage. It is bound up with it. The intimacy of marriage and the sacrament of marriage belong to one reality of covenantal self-gift.

Many Christians have never been taught this. Some were told that marriage is simply friendship and companionship. Others were told that sexual intimacy exists only for procreation, or perhaps for pleasure within certain limits. Yet the Catholic vision is far richer. The Church sees marital intimacy, rightly ordered, as part of the sanctifying life of the spouses. The Catechism says, "Sexuality is ordered to the conjugal love of man and woman" and "in marriage the physical intimacy of the spouses becomes a sign and pledge of spiritual communion" (CCC 2360). That is already much more than modern categories can hold.

So when we return to Genesis 3, the real question is not whether childbearing, work, marriage, or intimacy are themselves cursed. The question is what sin has done to the good things God originally made.

The Sorrow of Childbearing and the Wounding of a Good Gift

The usual English rendering says, "I will greatly multiply your pain in childbearing" (Gen 3:16). Yet the Hebrew term points beyond physical pain alone. It includes sorrow, grief, and anguish. Certainly, physical childbirth is painful. Every man with any sense should recognise that women bear a burden in childbirth beyond anything he can fully grasp. Yet the biblical curse goes deeper than labour pains. It includes the sorrow that sin brings into fruitfulness itself.

The blessing to be fruitful remains. God does not revoke the goodness of motherhood or the holiness of marital union. What is wounded is the experience of these gifts within a fallen world. The sorrow includes miscarriage, sickness, fear, vulnerability, anxiety, and the deep maternal anguish that accompanies the fragility of life after the fall. None of that belonged to Eden. None of that was part of the divine intention in creation. Sin did not erase the blessing. Sin invaded the experience of the blessing.

The mother bears this in a profound way. Her body and soul become the place where life is welcomed, sheltered, nourished, and then brought forth. The suffering of this vocation, after the fall, reaches deeply into the heart. Yet so too does its strength. There is something astonishingly resilient in the receptivity of woman. There is something in her spiritual and bodily constitution that remains oriented to life because the original blessing was spoken before sin and cannot be annulled by the serpent.

This is why the Church consistently defends the dignity of marriage, motherhood, and human fruitfulness against every ideology of use. Saint John Paul II wrote that woman has a particular "capacity for the other person," and that her vocation is bound up with a profound personal responsiveness to life and love (Mulieris Dignitatem, 18, 30). Sin wounds that vocation. Grace heals and elevates it.

Adam's Failure and the Curse on the Ground

The curse on Adam is just as revealing. The English translation says, "Because you have listened to the voice of your wife" (Gen 3:17). Yet the deeper sense is not that a husband sins merely by listening to his bride. That would be absurd. Scripture elsewhere commands attentiveness, mutuality, and wisdom in the covenantal life of husband and wife. The point is that Adam allowed himself to be influenced into disobedience when he should have been protecting, discerning, and guarding. He received from Eve what he should have corrected in Eve. He failed to intervene where he was meant to stand firm.

Then the Lord says, "Cursed is the ground because of you" (Gen 3:17). Here again the Hebrew depth matters. The curse reaches through Adam into the material order itself. Work, labour, agriculture, sweat, frustration, fatigue, and mortality all now bear the wound of human rebellion. The man was made to till and keep the garden (Gen 2:15). Labour itself was good before the fall. Yet after the fall it becomes drudgery. The vocation remains, though now afflicted.

This means that the fallen human experience of work is not merely tiring because human beings are lazy. It is tiring because creation itself has been subjected to disorder through sin. Saint Paul later writes that "the creation was subjected to futility" and that "the whole creation has been groaning in travail together until now" (Rom 8:20, 22). Genesis and Romans therefore meet in a single theology. Adam's sin wounds not only himself or his marriage, though those are central. It reaches into history, labour, and material reality.

The Easter Vigil proclaims not the happy fault of Eve, though she sinned, but "O happy fault… which gained for us so great a Redeemer." The tradition of the Church places the representative burden on Adam because covenant headship failed through him. Christ therefore comes as the New Adam. "For as by a man came death, by a man has come also the resurrection of the dead" (1 Cor 15:21). The remedy begins with Christ, and within marriage the husband is summoned to rediscover in Christ the truth of his office.

What Satan Could Not Curse

And yet here is the decisive point. Satan could not touch the goodness of marital intimacy itself.

He could wound the experience of it. He could distort the imagination around it. He could make the fruitfulness of marriage painful. He could introduce shame, lust, selfishness, and fear. He could tempt couples either toward impurity before marriage or toward coldness within marriage. Yet he could not make what God called good become evil in itself.

We see this immediately after the curse. Adam looks upon his bride and names her Eve, Havvah, "because she was the mother of all living" (Gen 3:20). This is an act of recognition and recovery. He is, as it were, trying to step back into his vocation as protector and provider. He names her according to the life that still flows through her. Motherhood remains holy. Fruitfulness remains holy. Marital union remains holy.

The Lord then makes garments of skin for them (Gen 3:21). Even this matters. God clothes their nakedness. He restores dignity where shame has entered. He does not abolish sexuality. He covers it in mercy and guards it in truth.

Then Genesis 4 begins with one of the most telling lines in Scripture: "And Adam knew Eve his wife, and she conceived and bore Cain" (Gen 4:1). The Hebrew verb is *yada*ʿ, to know. The sacred text does not reduce the act to mere mechanics. It speaks of knowing. Marital intimacy is bodily, yes, though also personal, spiritual, covenantal, and profoundly relational. Husband and wife know one another in a way that includes the body yet surpasses the merely physical. This alone should challenge the flattened language of modernity.

Marital Intimacy as Sign, Pledge, and Sanctifying Grace

The Catechism states, "Sexuality is ordered to the conjugal love of man and woman" and "in marriage the physical intimacy of the spouses becomes a sign and pledge of spiritual communion" (CCC 2360). It continues: "The sexual acts in marriage by which the intimate and chaste union of the spouses takes place are noble and honorable" (CCC 2362). Moreover, "the spouses' union achieves the twofold end of marriage: the good of the spouses themselves and the transmission of life" (CCC 2363).

This means that marital intimacy is not something outside grace. It is a place where sacramental grace is enacted, embodied, renewed, and deepened when lived according to God's design. The bonds of marriage between the baptised are sanctified (CCC 2360). Marital intimacy, therefore, can never be understood merely as appetite or release. It belongs within the sacramental life of the couple. It becomes a bodily language of covenant fidelity.

Saint John Paul II unfolded this magnificently in his catecheses later gathered as the Theology of the Body. He argued that the body has a spousal meaning. It is capable of expressing the gift of self. Within marriage, husband and wife speak through their bodies a language that must be truthful. The act says, in effect, I give myself entirely to you. I receive you entirely. I hold nothing back that belongs to the covenant. When that language is contradicted by selfishness, contraception, infidelity, domination, fantasy, pornography, or manipulation, the body is made to speak falsely.

This is why one can say, in a properly theological sense, that the marital embrace renews and embodies the vows. In bodily form the spouses say again what they said verbally at the altar. I am yours. I give myself to you. I receive you. I remain with you. John Paul II even drew Eucharistic resonances in this area, though always carefully and analogically. There is a profound bodily self-gift here that echoes, without equating, the words of Christ: "This is my body which is given for you" (Luke 22:19). Within marriage, each spouse becomes for the other a covenantal gift.

God in the Room

One of the great losses in modern Christian imagination is that many people can still believe that God was present at their wedding and absent from their bedroom. They can believe that he received their vows, witnessed their covenant, and blessed their union, though they then leave him outside the door when the embodied form of that covenant is lived.

That is a profound mistake.

God is not a voyeur. God is the author of marriage, the giver of the sacrament, the Lord of the covenant, and the source of grace within it. To say that God is present in marital intimacy is not to degrade the act. It is to restore it to its true dignity. The act is holy precisely because it belongs to God's design for covenant love. That is why pornography is such a blasphemous counterfeit. It rips a holy thing from its proper covenantal place and profanes it for consumption, detaching the body from personhood, gift, fruitfulness, and grace.

The Church Fathers often spoke with far more boldness on this topic than many modern Christians realise. Saint John Chrysostom, for instance, urged husbands to approach their wives with reverence, affection, spiritual intentionality, and eternal perspective. The early Church did not think the bedroom should be ruled by vulgarity, nor by embarrassment, nor by prudish silence. It thought it should be ruled by truth, holiness, and charity.

Fulton Sheen captured this with extraordinary precision. In essence, he argued that mere sexuality can become a mutual adoration of bodies, whereas true love becomes an adoration of God through the body of the beloved. That is exactly the difference between lust and charity, between use and gift, between profanation and sacrament.

The Song of Songs & the Language of Holy Desire

If anyone doubts how seriously God takes marital intimacy, he need only read the Song of Songs. The book is unabashedly nuptial. It follows, in many respects, the trajectory of Hebrew wedding imagery, covenant celebration, procession, desire, and consummation. It is at once a poem of bride and bridegroom, an allegory of God and Israel, and for Christians an image of Christ and the Church.

Listen to the language: "How sweet is your love, my sister, my bride" (Song 4:10). Or again: "A garden locked is my sister, my bride, a garden locked, a fountain sealed" (Song 4:12). Then the bride says, "Let my beloved come to his garden, and eat its choicest fruits" (Song 4:16).

The biblical imagination is not embarrassed by holy desire. It does not deny the reality of bodily attraction. Yet it places that desire within covenant, symbolism, fruitfulness, and mutual delight. The body is not reduced. It is elevated. The woman is not treated as an object. She is received as a mystery, gift, garden, sanctuary, and delight. The man is not treated as a consumer. He is addressed as beloved within covenantal love.

Contrast that with the vulgar reductionism of contemporary culture. The modern world speaks often of sex, though very rarely of intimacy, holiness, communion, fruitfulness, truth, tenderness, or covenant. It knows how to expose the body. It does not know how to reverence the person.

Scripture already gives us better language. The Church already gives us better categories. Married couples do not need the sexualised culture to teach them what intimacy means. The sexualised culture needs conversion by the Catholic vision of marriage.

Why the Devil Targets the Bed

Years ago, I encountered a striking insight from a priest involved in deliverance ministry. He observed that before marriage the devil works hard to get a man and woman into bed together. After marriage he works hard to keep them away from bed together. That line has remained with me because it is both simple and deeply perceptive.

Before marriage, Satan wants to strip the act of covenant. After marriage, he wants to strip the covenant of the act. In both cases he wants the same thing. He wants separation between what God has joined.

This is why marital intimacy must be seen as a site of spiritual warfare. Many couples do not think of it in those terms. Yet they should. Here Satan tempts by shame, fantasy, distraction, selfishness, resentment, insecurity, comparison, exhaustion, and silence. He wants couples suspicious of the act, careless about the act, divided in the act, or entirely estranged from the act. Why? Because he knows what it means. He knows that when husband and wife come together in truth, charity, openness to life, and sacramental integrity, grace is at work.

Ten Ways Satan Attacks Marital Intimacy

What follows are ten recurring patterns by which marital intimacy is often attacked in our time.

1. Shame and disgust

There is a strange social script whereby even saying the word sex can make Christians cringe, though the reality itself is already known to them. This reveals a cultural formation of embarrassment rather than a theological formation of reverence. Marital intimacy is private, though it need not be shameful.

2. Lust replacing love

Love wills the good of the other. Lust makes the other an instrument of the self. If a couple begins to approach intimacy through entitlement, appetite, or emotional consumption, then the logic of gift has been compromised.

3. Pornography and fantasy

This is a massive wound in the modern imagination. Aquinas teaches that what enters the imagination shapes the inner life and the passions. If the imagination is saturated with impurity, that disordered imagery will be carried into marriage unless it is purified by grace, confession, discipline, and healing.

4. Contraceptive mentality

When the act is deliberately severed from its procreative meaning, the body is made to say less than the covenant means. The Church insists that the unitive and procreative meanings of the act must remain joined (Humanae Vitae, 12; CCC 2366–2370). This is true even when age or infertility make conception naturally impossible, because the structure of the act itself must still honour the truth of the body.

5. Selfishness and entitlement

When one spouse prioritises personal gratification rather than mutual self-gift, dissatisfaction follows. The act was designed for reciprocal charity, not consumption.

6. Resentment and unresolved conflict

Emotional wounds do not remain neatly compartmentalised. They enter the bodily life of the marriage. This is why unresolved anger, bitterness, or alienation can deeply affect intimacy. Saint Paul's exhortation remains urgent: "Do not let the sun go down on your anger" (Eph 4:26).

7. Power games and domination

Genesis 3:16 warns that fallen relations between man and woman can become distorted by domination. The husband must never use strength as control. The wife must never manipulate through withdrawal or humiliation. The covenant is ordered to mutual self-gift, not domination.

8. Busyness and distraction

Work, children, fatigue, travel, ministry, and good obligations can still crowd out the marriage if a couple ceases to make deliberate space for intimacy. Desire does not always lead effort. Often, in mature marriages, effort leads desire.

9. Insecurity and comparison

   This often affects women particularly, though men as well. Wounds from comparison, ageing, pornography, silence, and emotional neglect can create distance. Husbands should therefore learn to say clearly and often that they still want their wives, still delight in them, and still receive them with joy.

10. Isolation and secrecy

    When difficulties are never addressed, patterns form. Days become weeks, weeks become months, and avoidance hardens into a settled structure. Silence gives the enemy too much room to work.

These attacks are real. Yet they are not final. Grace is stronger.

Purifying the Imagination

What, then, is the answer?

First, the imagination must be purified. Many people need healing in how they think about marital intimacy. They need Scripture to teach them again. They need the sacraments to heal memory. They need confession to break chains. They need spiritual disciplines to retrain habits. They may need sound Catholic resources that explain both the theology and the moral life of marriage with practical wisdom.

The heart cannot sustain holy marital intimacy when the imagination has been catechised by pornography, consumerism, comparison, and self-reference. Therefore prayer matters. Confession matters. Honest conversation matters. Reading good Catholic teaching matters. The Eucharist matters.

The Catechism teaches that the grace of the sacrament of Matrimony is given "to perfect the couple's love and to strengthen their indissoluble unity" (CCC 1641). That grace is not abstract. It is meant to shape habits, speech, tenderness, desire, healing, discipline, and sacrifice.

Marital Intimacy and the Renewal of Vows

The deepest truth here is simple. Marital intimacy, lived in truth, becomes a bodily renewal of covenant fidelity. In that sense it renews the vows. Husband and wife once promised, "I will love you in good times and in bad, in sickness and in health, all the days of my life." Within the marital embrace, they embody that promise. The body says what the soul vowed.

This is why one may rightly say that marital intimacy can be a renewal of sanctifying grace in the life of the spouses, not because it is a separate sacrament, though because it belongs intrinsically to the sacrament they already received. It is the sacrament lived, enacted, and embodied. It is covenant speech through the body.

John Paul II insisted that the language of the body must be spoken in truth. When it is, the spouses are not merely exchanging pleasure. They are exchanging themselves. They are practising charity in embodied form. They are receiving one another again. They are, in that sense, becoming more fully what they vowed to be.

Go Be Saints

Let us be direct. The sexualised culture has given counterfeit categories. It has made holy things vulgar and vulgar things ordinary. It has trained many Christians to be embarrassed by what God sanctified and casual about what God judges. Yet the Church still teaches a radiant vision.

Marriage is holy. The body is holy. Marital intimacy is holy. The act by which husband and wife become one flesh is noble, honourable, and sanctifiable when lived according to God's order. It is ordered to union. It is ordered to life. It is ordered to self-gift. It is ordered to grace.

So husbands and wives should pray for the purification of their imagination, the healing of their habits, the restoration of tenderness, and the courage to fight where Satan attacks. They should remember that grace is available here too. They should remember that Christ redeems not only the public dimensions of life, though also the hidden ones. He enters even the most intimate chambers of the covenant he established.

And so this prayer is fitting:

Father, I thank you for the way you designed man and woman. I thank you for the way you designed marriage. I thank you for the way you designed marital intimacy. I thank you for the lofty goal you created for what marriage and marital intimacy ought to be. I thank you that you have made marital intimacy between bride and bridegroom a channel through which the marital vows are renewed and sanctifying grace is deepened. Purify our imagination. Purify our thoughts. Purify our habits. Purify the way we approach our spouses. Heal what is distorted. Strengthen what is weak. Restore what has grown cold. Teach us to become saints together.

For this is the truth. Husband and wife are not merely meant to endure marriage. They are meant to be sanctified in it. They are meant to become one flesh in truth, one heart in charity, and one household in grace. Amen.

So then, my friends, go be saints.

Meditation Questions

1. Do I view marital intimacy primarily through cultural categories, or through God's plan as

revealed in Scripture and the Church's teaching?

2. Have I allowed shame, embarrassment, or silence to keep me from reverencing the holiness of marital intimacy?
3. In what ways has selfishness, entitlement, resentment, or emotional distance affected intimacy in my marriage?
4. Have pornography, fantasy, comparison, or impurity wounded my imagination and my way of seeing my spouse?
5. Do I believe that marital intimacy, rightly ordered, is part of God's sanctifying grace in our marriage?
6. Have I treated my spouse as a gift, or have I subtly treated my spouse as a means of meeting my needs?
7. What practical obstacles are keeping us from tenderness, unity, honesty, and healing in this area of our marriage?

Call to Action

This week, schedule one intentional, private conversation with your spouse specifically about intimacy, purity, and unity. Begin by praying together for purity of mind, healing of memory, and deeper trust before discussing anything else.

Marriage Checkpoint Questionnaire

Instructions

Here is a 25-question marriage checkpoint designed for a husband and wife to work through together. It is meant to be an honest, practical, and spiritual help. It works well as an occasional review.

You may grab a piece of paper and number 1-25 and answer each question with:

1 = rarely true
2 = sometimes true
3 = often true
4 = consistently true

After scoring, discuss your answers together one by one. Don't merely tally the numbers.

Marriage Checkpoint

A Couple's Shared Examination of Covenant Life

Christ at the Center

1. We are intentionally placing Christ at the center of our marriage rather than expecting each other to be what only God can be.
2. We pray for each other regularly and sincerely.
3. We pray with each other in some consistent way.
4. We encourage one another toward confession, the Eucharist, and holiness.

Communication and Emotional Unity

5. We speak honestly with each other about what is happening in our hearts.
6. We listen to each other without becoming quickly defensive.
7. We are able to discuss difficult topics without contempt, mockery, or shutting down.

8. We make each other feel emotionally safe when fears, wounds, or frustrations are expressed.

Love, Tenderness, and Affection

9. We are deliberate about expressing affection in words and actions.
10. We make each other feel wanted, cherished, and seen.
11. We are still dating each other in some real way rather than merely managing a household together.
12. We are attentive to the little acts of love that matter to the other person.

Conflict and Reconciliation

13. We apologise clearly when we fail rather than giving vague or defensive apologies.
14. We forgive each other sincerely and work against storing resentment.
15. We do not allow past hurts to become the constant lens through which we interpret one another.

16. When conflict happens, we try to bring it to prayer and resolution rather than avoidance and silence.

Intimacy and Purity

17. We see marital intimacy as holy, unitive, and part of our covenant life.
18. We are able to discuss intimacy honestly, respectfully, and without shame.
19. We are guarding our marriage against pornography, fantasy, secrecy, or comparison.
20. We are making a real effort to remain tender, self-giving, and united in this part of our marriage.

Shared Life and Mission

21. We are working as a team in the practical demands of marriage, family life, and responsibilities.
22. We are protecting our marriage from unhealthy third-party intrusions, whether emotional, relational, digital, or familial.

23. We are united in the way we think about our home, our children, and the kind of family culture we want to build.
24. We are helping each other become saints rather than merely helping each other get through the week.
25. At this point in our marriage, I can honestly say that our covenant is growing, deepening, and becoming more heavenly.

Notes on How to Use It Together

Step 1: Fill It Out Separately

Each spouse should answer every question alone first.

Step 2: Compare Gently

When you come together, do not begin with the lowest scores. Go one question at a time.

Step 3: Discuss the Gaps

Pay close attention to questions where your scores differ by 2 points or more. Those usually reveal blind spots, hurts, or unmet needs.

Step 4: Choose 3 Priorities

Do not try to fix everything at once. Choose:

- one spiritual priority
- one relational priority
- one practical priority

Step 5: Make One Concrete Commitment Each

Each spouse should complete this sentence:

"This week, one concrete way I will love you better is…"

Reflection Prompts After the Questionnaire

You may also ask each other these five follow-up questions:

1. Where do you feel most loved by me right now?
2. Where do you feel most alone or unseen by me right now?
3. What is one thing I do that brings you peace?
4. What is one thing I do that creates distance between us?
5. What is one specific grace you want us to ask God for together?

Simple Scoring Guide

You do not need to obsess over the number, but as a rough guide:

- ***85–100: strong foundation, though still in need of continued intentionality***
- ***65–84: generally healthy, though there are a few important areas to address***

- ***45–64: several weak points need prayerful and practical attention***
- ***Below 45: your marriage likely needs immediate, serious, and sustained intervention with prayer, sacramental grace, and wise support***

Final Question

End by asking each other:

> "What would help you most right now to experience our marriage more as a path to heaven?"

And then pray together before you leave the conversation.

www.ingramcontent.com/pod-product-compliance
Lightning Source LLC
LaVergne TN
LVHW040221110826
845146LV00005B/1369

* 9 7 9 8 8 8 8 7 0 5 3 8 4 *